Contents

Match three-digit numbers to words	2–3
Know what each digit represents in a three-digit number	4–5
Find the value of a digit in a three-digit number	6–7
Find ten more/one hundred more than a number (0–999)	8–9
Find ten less/one hundred less than a number (0–999)	10–11
Find numbers to match divisions on a number line (0–100)	12–13
Find the previous odd/even number	14–15
Find one more/one less than a number (0–999)	16–17
Recognise simple fractions	18–19
Find a number between two numbers (0–999)	20–21
Develop mathematical vocabulary	22
Solve money problems	23
Solve number problems involving number sequences	24

Find words to match the numbers.

1	2	3	4
725	803	917	664

5	6	7	8
542	731	713	646

9	10	11	12
752	524	971	830

SIX HUNDRED 650 AND FIFTY

six hundred and forty-six	eight hundred and thirty	five hundred and twenty-four	seven hundred and thirteen	nine hundred and seventy-one	five hundred and forty-two
eight hundred and three	seven hundred and thirty-one	seven hundred and twenty-five	six hundred and sixty-four	seven hundred and fifty-two	nine hundred and seventeen

 Which of these numbers is the largest?
Which of these numbers is the smallest?

Find the value of the coloured digit in the position shown.

1. 67**3**	2. **8**61	3. 12**9**	4. 8**9**2
5. 54**8**	6. 33**2**	7. **9**18	8. 7**3**4
9. 2**8**6	10. 2**2**5	11. **2**09	12. **3**07

4

| 9 | 80 | 90 | 3 | 2 | 800 |
| 8 | 200 | 900 | 20 | 300 | 30 |

Find pairs of numbers in which one is 10 times the other.
Find pairs of numbers in which one is 100 times the other.

Find the missing number.

1	2	3	4	5	6
425	755	362	632	477	249
400 + [ ] + 5	700 + [ ] + 5	300 + [ ] + 2	600 + [ ] + 2	400 + [ ] + 7	200 + [ ] + 9
7	8	9	10	11	12
277	351	517	716	983	642
[ ] + 70 + 7	[ ] + 50 + 1	[ ] + 10 + 7	[ ] + 10 + 6	[ ] + 80 + 3	[ ] + 40 + 2

500 + 60 + 5 = 565

| 900 | 60 | 20 | 30 | 50 | 600 |
| 500 | 70 | 700 | 200 | 300 | 40 |

 Which of these numbers can you divide by 10?

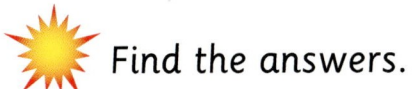 Find the answers.

1) 36 +10 → ?	2) 57 +10 → ?	3) 81 +10 → ?	7) 36 +100 → ?	8) 57 +100 → ?	9) 81 +100 → ?
4) 125 +10 → ?	5) 276 +10 → ?	6) 518 +10 → ?	10) 125 +100 → ?	11) 276 +100 → ?	12) 518 +100 → ?

| 91 | 376 | 135 | 46 | 618 | 67 |
| 286 | 181 | 136 | 225 | 528 | 157 |

What is 10 more than each number?
What is 100 more than each number?

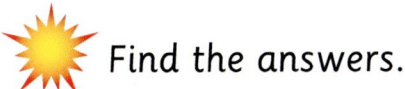 Find the answers.

1. 253 −10→ ?	2. 317 −10→ ?	3. 426 −10→ ?	7. 353 −100→ ?	8. 317 −100→ ?	9. 426 −100→ ?
4. 736 −10→ ?	5. 680 −10→ ?	6. 901 −10→ ?	10. 736 −100→ ?	11. 680 −100→ ?	12. 901 −100→ ?

| 580 | 416 | 253 | 636 | 307 | 801 |
| 326 | 670 | 726 | 243 | 217 | 891 |

What is 10 less than each number?
What is 100 less than each number?

Look carefully at the start and end numbers. To which number does the arrow point?

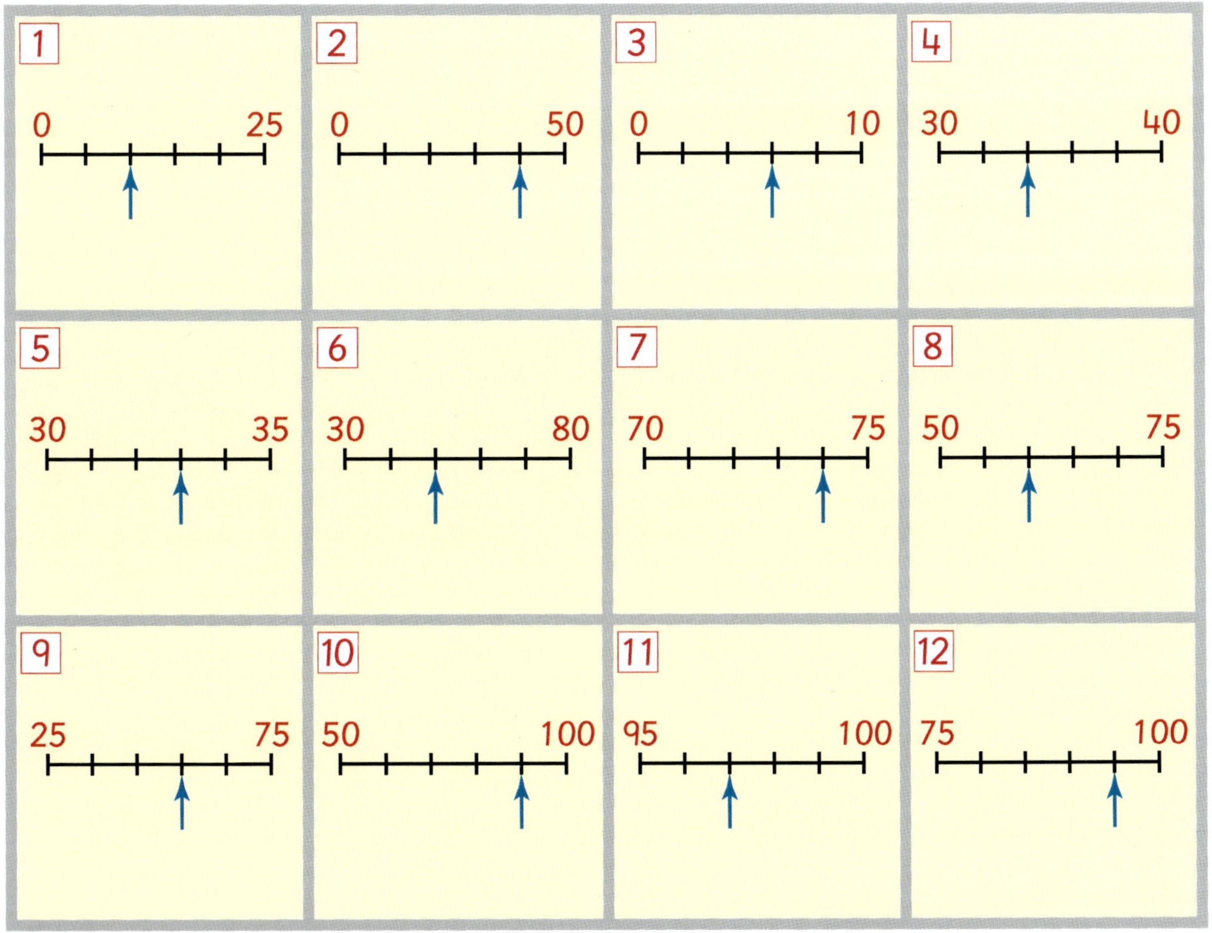

1	0 — 25	2	0 — 50	3	0 — 10	4	30 — 40
5	30 — 35	6	30 — 80	7	70 — 75	8	50 — 75
9	25 — 75	10	50 — 100	11	95 — 100	12	75 — 100

| 95 | 40 | 6 | 55 | 34 | 90 |
| 50 | 60 | 33 | 97 | 74 | 10 |

Which of these numbers is the largest even number?
Which of these numbers is the smallest odd number?

Which **even** number comes **before** each of these?

1. 48
2. 66
3. 70
4. 82
5. 94
6. 30

Which **odd** number comes **before** each of these?

7. 47
8. 65
9. 69
10. 81
11. 93
12. 29

| 91 | 92 | 46 | 80 | 63 | 27 |
| 67 | 68 | 79 | 45 | 64 | 28 |

Which of these numbers are greater than 75?
Which of these numbers are less than 50?

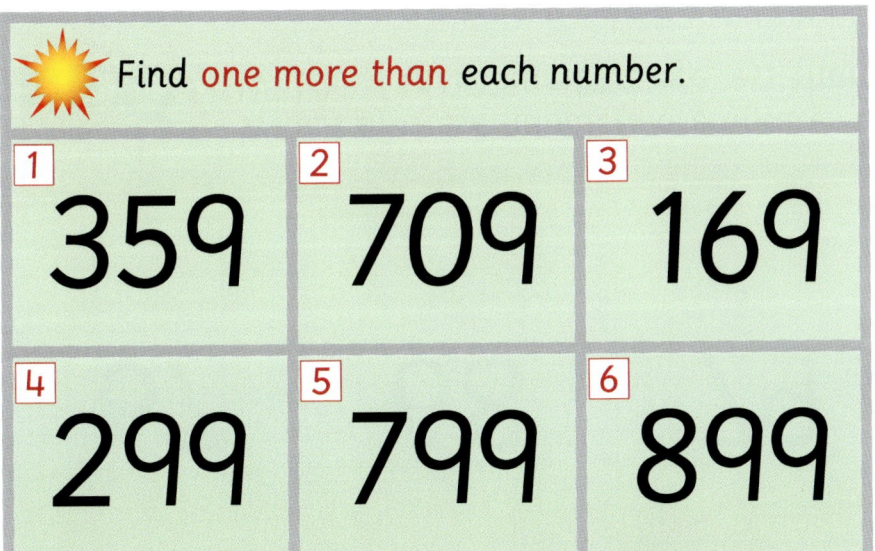

Find **one more than** each number.

1. 359
2. 709
3. 169
4. 299
5. 799
6. 899

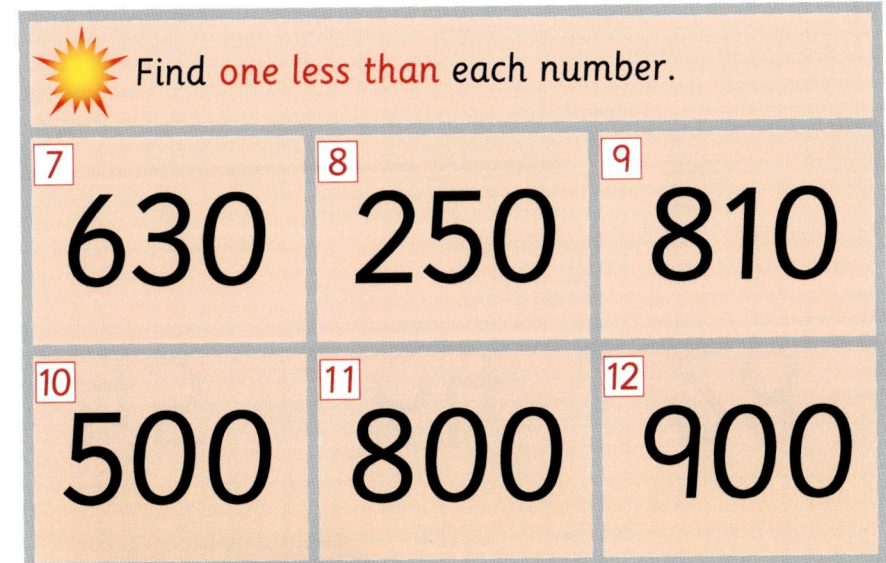

Find **one less than** each number.

7. 630
8. 250
9. 810
10. 500
11. 800
12. 900

501

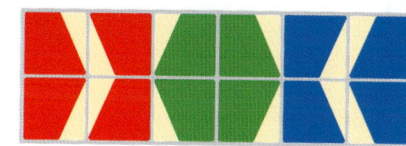

170	799	360	300	900	249
800	809	499	629	899	710

What is 1 more than each number?
What is 1 less than each number?

Look at the coloured part. Find the matching fraction.

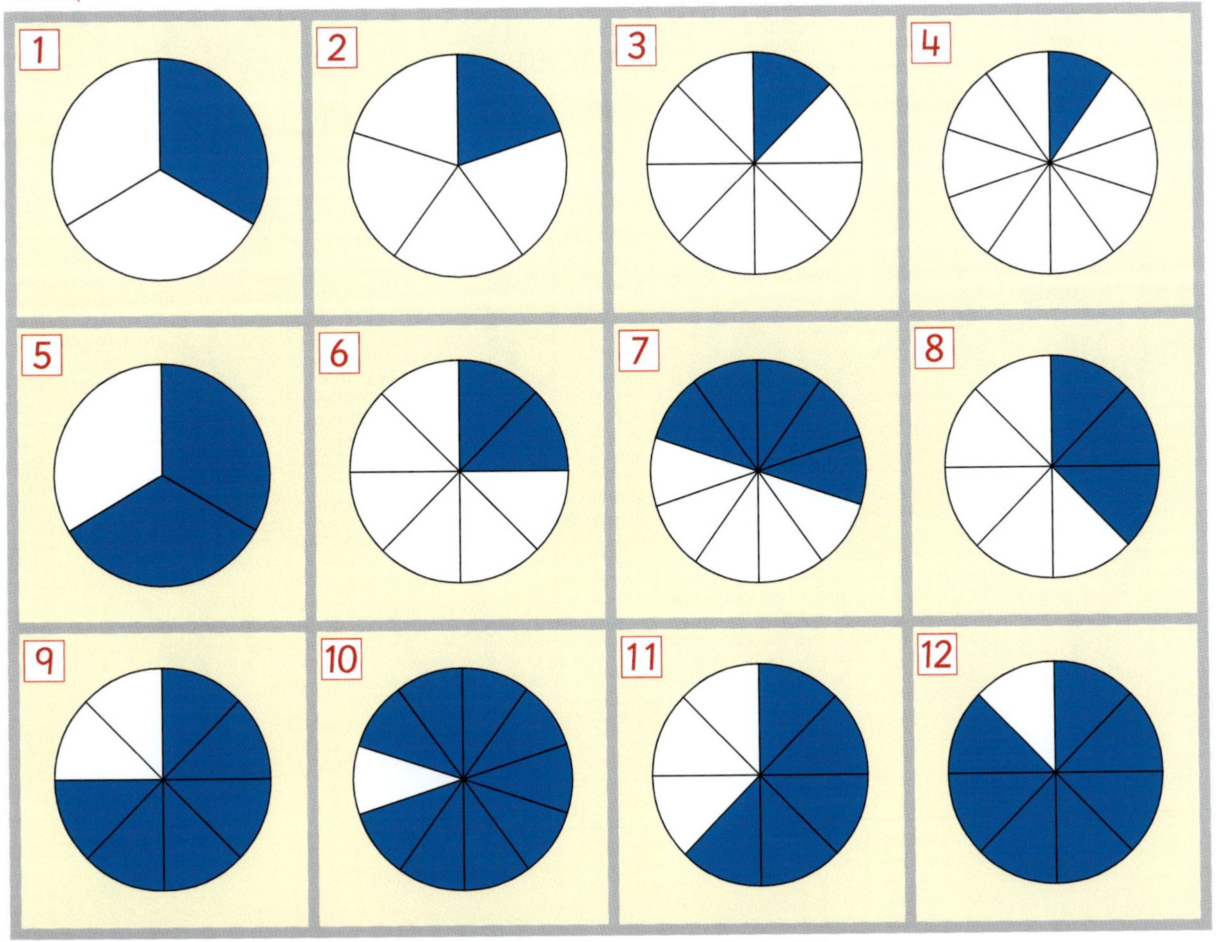

18

$\frac{5}{8}$	$\frac{2}{3}$	$\frac{1}{10}$	$\frac{1}{3}$	$\frac{3}{8}$	$\frac{7}{8}$
$\frac{3}{4}$	$\frac{1}{8}$	$\frac{1}{2}$	$\frac{9}{10}$	$\frac{1}{5}$	$\frac{1}{4}$

 Which of the fractions is the largest?
Which of the fractions is the smallest?

Find a number that goes *between* each pair. The three numbers must be in order.

1. 722 ? 726
2. 728 ? 732
3. 740 ? 745
4. 738 ? 742
5. 731 ? 736
6. 734 ? 739
7. 752 ? 754
8. 755 ? 760
9. 766 ? 771
10. 772 ? 776
11. 763 ? 766
12. 778 ? 783

| 738 | 759 | 744 | 767 | 753 | 725 |
| 779 | 729 | 733 | 764 | 740 | 775 |

 Which number is 100 more than each of these?
Which number is 100 less than each of these?

 Find the answer to match each question.

1	What is a half of 18?	20	1
2	What is a quarter of 20?	6	2
3	What is a third of 12?	68	3
4	What is a fifth of 15?	30	4
5	What is a tenth of 60?	45	5
6	Which is the odd number immediately before 51?	49	6
7	Which is the even number immediately before 70?	60	7
8	What is the multiple of 5 immediately after 40?	4	8
9	What is the multiple of 5 immediately before 25?	3	9
10	What is the multiple of 10 immediately after 20?	9	10
11	What is the multiple of 10 immediately before 70?	5	11
12	What is the multiple of 2 immediately after 14?	16	12

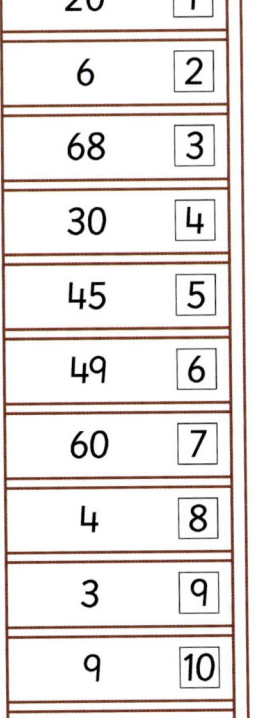

Find the answer to match each question.

1	Which is more, £4.20 or £4.02?
2	Which is less, £4.02 or £4.50?
3	What is 10p more than £2.90?
4	What is 10p less than £5.00?
5	Which amount is half of £1?
6	Which amount is £1 more than £2.50?
7	Which amount is £1 less than £2.50?
8	What is double £2.50?
9	What is half of £5.00?
10	How much more is £1 than £0.01?
11	What is the difference between £1 and £0.10?
12	What must be added to £0.90 to make £1?

- £2.50   1
- £3.00   2
- £0.99   3
- £1.50   4
- £4.02   5
- £3.50   6
- £0.90   7
- £0.50   8
- £4.20   9
- £4.90   10
- £5.00   11
- £0.10   12

 Find the answer to match each question.

#	Question	Answer
1	What is 67 rounded to the nearest 10?	20 — 1
2	What is 86 rounded to the nearest 10?	90 — 2
3	What is 144 rounded to the nearest 100?	70 — 3
4	What is 555 rounded to the nearest 100?	600 — 4
5	Which is the larger, 750 or 570?	100 — 5
6	Which multiple of 50 follows 150?	30 — 6
7	Which multiple of 100 follows 400?	200 — 7
8	Which multiple of 10 lies between 560 and 580?	570 — 8
9	Counting in 4s, what comes next after 76?	60 — 9
10	Counting in 3s, what comes next after 57?	500 — 10
11	What is the sixth multiple of 5?	750 — 11
12	What is the tenth multiple of 2?	80 — 12

24